COLOURS GUIDE

MUSEUMS

HOUSE OF THE KING

PANTHEONS

MONASTERY

BASILICA

LIBRARY

COLLEGE

MAIN FAÇADE

PALACE OF THE BOURBONS

GARDENS

Main floor

Ground floor

Basement

1 MUSEUMS
  A St.Maurice Hall
  B Architecture museum
  C Museum of Art

2 PATIO OF MASKS

3 THE GALLERY OF BATTLES

4 THE HOUSE OF THE KING

5 THE PANTHEONS

6 THE CHAPTER HOUSES

7 THE MAIN CLOISTER
  A The Patio of the Evangelists

8 THE MAIN STAIRCASE

9 THE OLD CHURCH

10 THE SACRISTY

11 THE BASILICA

12 PATIO OF KINGS

13 THE LIBRARY

14 THE MAIN FAÇADE

15 THE PALACE OF THE BOURBONS

VISITOR'S GUIDE

MONASTERY
OF
SAN LORENZO EL REAL
DE
EL ESCORIAL

José Luis Sancho

© ALDEASA ® : 1994

Legal Deposit : M-7209-1997

I.S.B.N.: 84-8003-040-2

I.S.B.N.: 84-7120-208-5

N.I.P.O. 006-97-002-5

Desing and Layout: Juan Manuel Dominguez

General Coordinator: Rose Mayer

Traslation: SAT /C.B.

Photographs: Patrimonio Nacional and Juan Manuel Dominguez*

Photomechanical Production: Megachrom, S.A., Eurocolor.

Cover illustration: copy of Juan de Herrera's seventh desing
by Johannes Blaeu in 1672.
Documentary research and photographic laboratory
production: Biblioteca Nacional.

Printed in Spain by: Estudios Gráficos Europeos, S.A. - Madrid

Fourth edition: february 1997

(Printed in Spain)

INDEX

View of the Monastery from the Abantos mountain.*

INTRODUCTION

The El Escorial Monastery is the monument which best represents the ideological and cultural aspirations of the "Spanish Golden Age". During this era , the Spanish Crown, which was the leading world power not only for its dynastic alliances and resulting territorial power in Europe, but also for its control of over almost all of the recently discovered American continent, established itself as the main defender of the Catholic Counter-Reformation as opposed to those countries which had embraced the Protestant Reform.

The "Catholic" King's struggle for European hegemony, the defense of the traditional religion, and the worship of dynasty and of the Monarch as one of God's chosen people, are strongly reflected in El Escorial by its original combination of Italian and Flemish artistic forms.

Nowadays, El Escorial continues under the royal trust of H.M. the King and its management and tutelage is dealt with by the National Patrimony.

THE FOUNDATION

San Lorenzo el Real was originally designed for a variety of purposes: as a monastery for the monks of the order of St. Jerome, whose church was the pantheon of Emperor Charles V, and of his wife, his son, Philip II, his relatives and heirs, and where the monks prayed endlessly for the salvation of the royal family; as a palace to house the King, patron of the foundation, and his entourage; the college and seminary complete the religious function of the Monastery, while the Library complements these three focal points.

The victory over Henry II of France in *Saint Quentin,* the first conquest in Philip II's reign, coincided with San Lorenzo Holy Day on August 10th, 1557. This led, in part, to the naming of the Monastery, which is not simply a votive monument.

Charles V also played a part in the Monastery's foundation given the enormous influence he had over his son's spirit, which can be seen by Philip II's wish to give his father a dignified burial after Charles V had spent his last years among the Hieronymite monks of Yuste.

THE FOUNDER

Philip II was King of Naples, Sicily and Milan from 1554, and King of the Netherlands a year later when a series of cessions were made by his father, Emperor Charles V, who retired to the Monastery of Yuste in 1556 and passed on the Crown of Spain and the New World to his son before he died in 1558.

THE WORK

Having decided to build the Monastery, Philip II began his search of the ideal site in 1558, which he finally located in 1562. Work began on the project or "universal design" drawn up by Juan Bautista de Toledo. By 1571, the Monastery area was almost complete; work commenced on the King's House in 1572 and on the Basilica in 1574, which was consecrated in 1595, the year in which most agree the Monastery was completed. Nonetheless, although the last stone was placed in 1584, a few more years were spent on its decoration. The King personally supervised all of the construction, responsibility for which fell to the architect, the prior and two commissions.

The architect was directly named by the King. As such, he only answered to Philip II and not to the prior, who was considered the maximum authority by everone else and who headed the "Congregation", the executive commission in charge of judicial and financial affairs, inspections and payments.

The northern façade, with the College's tower and "la lonja".*

THE ARTISANS

El Escorial can by no means be considered the work of a single architect, but the product of close collaboration between two men: Juan Bautista de Toledo and Juan de Herrera. Juan Bautista de Toledo, who had worked under Michelangelo in the Vatican, was charged with drawing up plans for the main body of the Monastery and most of the

General view of the Monastery
from the House of the Infante.[*]

General view of the Monastery and the gardens from the South.*

designs. Juan de Herrera was responsible for the completion of the complex, including several parts of the buiding which had not been designed by Toledo. If one takes into account further contributions to the building by several other Spanish and Italian architects, then the final result of El Escorial must be seen as a very personal manifestation of Philip II's character.

Neither must one forget the contribution made by the master builders and the overseers, such as Brother Antonio de Villacastín, Pedro de Tolosa, Diego de Alcántara or Juan de Minjares. Francisco de Mora was a disciple of Herrera who continued this architect's work from 1583 onwards. In the 18th century, the spirit of El Escorial shaped the classically Italian-trained Juan de Villanueva's work on the major projects he carried out on the Monastery for Charles III and Charles IV.

The Gardens of the King and the monks in front of the Eastern façade.

The main façade of the Monastery.

La Lonja and the Northern façade.*

EL ESCORIAL FROM THE 16TH TO THE 19TH CENTURIES

The Institution remained faithful to the desires and plans of its founder until 1835, and was enriched by the contributions made by the succeeding monarchs.

Philip III began work on the *Pantheon.* Philip IV completed it and enhanced its collection of paintings with some major works. Charles II had Bartolomé Zumbigo rebuilt the Monastery after it burned down in 1671, and redecorate it with a *retable* of the Sacristy and a series of grandiose *frescoes* by Luca Giordano. From 1767 onwards, Charles III ordered a residential area to be built in Real Sitio, with the new houses of "la Lonja" and the two *"little houses of pleasure"* for the Prince and his brother. Charles IV had the northern façade remodelled and the Palace of the Bourbons decorated.

EL ESCORIAL IN THE 19TH AND 20TH CENTURIES

The disentailing laws of the 19th century obliged the community of Hieronymite monks to abandon the Monastery and led to the channelling of the foundation's wealth to the Patrimony of the Crown. The Monastery was then destined for use by different religions until the Augustinian monks appeared

View of the Southern façade of
the Monastery, with the Gallery
of the Convalescents and the
garden pool.*

in 1885. The IV Centennial celebrations from 1963 to 1984-1986 commemorating the placing of the first and last stones sparked off a new phase of restoration and studies on the Real Sitio.

THE VISIT

The San Lorenzo el Real Monastery of El Escorial consists of a huge rectangle within which the following areas designed for separate functions are distributed:

The sacred area of the Church and its atrium.
The Monastery, laid out around one big and four small patios.
The House of the King.
The outbuildings of the Palace of the King.
The College.
The Library.

This "universal design" drawn up by Juan Bautista de Toledo is influenced the cross-shaped floor plans of 15th century Italian and Spanish hospitals, but it is generally thought that its main inspiration comes from the traditional layout of medieval monasteries.

The Monastery is situated on the mountain side, orientated towards the four cardinal points, with the altar facing East in such a way that this and the South side, where the land slopes down, are enclosed by gardens supported by thick walls. The Northern and Western sides, where the land is higher, are surrounded by an area of deference called *"la Lonja"* (the Porch).

If you approach the Monastery by the Galapagar road, the most picturesque view of the building can be seen, with the House of the King, the rear of the Basilica and its dome. You can only reach the *main Façade* by crossing "la Lonja" and encircling the whole building. The Monastery is impressive for its uniformity and lack of ornamentation, with each façade conserving its own individual character.

Juan Bautista de Toledo did not originally plan for so much uniformity. He imagined the western part of the building with one floor less and towers in

the centres of the northern and southern façades giving it much more height. The variation in the building's forms would have given it a harmonious style more in keeping with the late Renaissance. Philip II decided to double the number of monks in the Monastery community to one hundred instead of fifty, and thus raised the whole building to four floors.

The two *Workers' Houses* are situated opposite the northern façade. Remodelled in the 18th century by Juan de Villanueva, they were built by Juan de Herrera in the 16th century to lodge the King's servants, and later joined to the Palace in 1769 by an *underground passage*, built by Brother Antonio Pontones, to protect the royal attendants' wigs and three-cornered hats from

The main entrance to the Monastery and the Chemist's tower.*

the strong winds. The *Compaña* to the south-west of "la Lonja" and constructed at the end of the 16th century by Francisco de Mora for the monks' servants is joined to the Monastery by a gallery built on arches.

Up until Charles III's reign, there were no buildings of any significance around the Monastery: the main façade faced the mountain in an exchange of Nature and Art. The Hieronymite monks lived like hermits and dedicated their time to prayer in the midst of the wilderness.

The other buildings that close off "la Lonja", are therefore, the work of Juan de Villanueva in the 18th century. Next to the Compaña, the *Houses of the Infantes* or King's children, begun in 1771 and, at an angle to this building, the *State Minister's House* both have splendid staircases.

1 THE MUSEUMS

The entrance door to the Museums is situated in the centre of the northern façade. This door used to give direct access to the Palace kitchens and are now the cafeteria and ticket offices. Once you have your ticket, you enter the *Patio of the Palace* or *carriages* from the doorway.

It is only possible to appreciate its full size from the main floor as half of the building is taken up by a T-shaped two-storey block which used to lodge the kitchen staff.
The rooms to the East and North of the Patio of carriages (or the Palace) form the *Palace of the Bourbons*. During the epoch of the Austrias, the northern rooms were taken by the ladies and gentlemen of the Court, and the eastern rooms were used by the King's children.

The entrance to the *New Museums* is located in the centre of the eastern gallery.

A ST. MAURICE HALL

The coloured wooden carving of *St. Michael triumphant over Lucifer,* by the Palace sculptress, Luisa Roldán, and important tapestries of the Golden Cloth series and that of the Temptations of Saint Anthony.

The Greco : *The Martyrdom of St. Maurice and the Theban Legion.* *

Model of one of the chapiters
of the towers.*

Tools for masonry and for the
art of hewing stone.*

On show in the second room is the splendid painting by Domenico Theotokopuli, *The Martyrdom of St. Maurice and the Theban Legion.*

Philip II did not like the El Greco painting he had ordered for an altar in the Basilica (it was later replaced by a work by Romulo Cincinnato) for "decorative" reasons or because its holy images did not conform to Counter-Reformation art.

Behind the El Greco painting, there is a stairway which leads down to the Monastery's *Museum of Architecture.*

☐
☐
■ **B** ARCHITECTURE MUSEUM

These halls, which were opened in 1963, and recently added to as a result of the IV Centennial exhibitions celebrated for the end of the Monastery's construction in 1986, constituted a didactic setting with sketches, scale models and other objects that explain by themselves the architectural design of El Escorial, from its prior medieval times, up to the new construction erected in the Royal Site during the XVIII Century, as well as the artisan aspects of the different trades implicated in its construction.

Hall 1: The precedents of the Monastery's "idea".

Hall 2: Juan Bautista de Toledo. The choice of this architect who was Spanish but have reached an elevated formation in Rome, being Michael Angelo's helper at the Vatican, and showing later his capacity in Naples, Phillip the II chose a style, since Juan Bautista de Toledo was the ideal person to introduce in Spain the vitruvian architecture which will represent a new Counter Reformed classicism.

Hall 3: Juan de Herrera, After Toledo's death continue with his well defined organization, the Factory's control, showing in outline, every time with bigger strenght, the figure of Juan de Herrera as a succesor and heir of the master. The sketches designed by Herrera and engraved by P. Perret offer a definite and more diffused image of the building finished by 1584.

Hall 4: The development of the project, the designs preserved at the Library of the Royal Palace in Madrid, of which some reproductionsare are here exhibeted, show aspects like the evolution of ideas for the Church from Juan Bautista to Herrera, or to the variations that he introduced in the other one's project.

Hall 5: The staircase and the main facade as well as other details from the building. El Escorial and the Spanish architecture of the XVI and XVII Centuries.

Hall 6: El Escorial and the Spanish architectural culture of the XVIII Century. Scale models and original pieces preserved of the "Monument" for the Holy Thursday.

Models of cranes used in the construction of the Monastery.*

Halls from 7 to 11: Here are reflected the technical aspects of the construction in five halls dedicated to the tools (7), the materials (8), the carpentry (9), the iron work and pumbling (10) and the machines (11).

From the Architecture Museum we pass to the Museum of Art.

☐
■   **C** MUSEUM OF ART
☐

The Museum of Art is located in the halls below the *House of the King*, that is the so-called *Summer Palace*, which were renovated in 1963 to exhibit those paintings amassed in the Monastery over the centuries that were not transferred to the Prado Museum in the 19th and 20th centuries. The Museum is set out as follows, taking notice that in summer it goes directly from hall 3 to 7 visiting 6,5, and 4 in this order at the end of the visit.

(1) Along with paintings from the 16th century Venetian school, the first room brings together other fine examples such as the magnificent *St. Michael* by Luca Cambiasso.

The Venetian works worth noting are: *St. Margaret* by Tiziano; *The Magdalen* by Tintoretto; and *The Eternal Father* by Paolo Veronese, whose studio was responsible for *The Descent,* a reduced version of which, painted by his son, Carlo Veronese, is also exhibited in this room.

(2) The second room is dedicated to Flemish art from the 16th and 17th centuries.

From the 16th century, there are two major works: *The Seven Liberal Arts* by Martin de Vos and *The Judgement of Solomon* by Pieter Aertsen, the latter dated 1562. From the 17th century, some fine examples are *The Supper of Emaus* by Rubens; Van Dyk's a *Virgin* and *Flight to Egypt* and *The Martyrdom of St. Justine,* painted by Giordano in the style of Rubens.

(3) The third room is entirely dedicated to the Italian-schooled Flemish painter, Miguel Coxcie, who worked a lot for Philip II.

(4)(5)(6) The three interior rooms, (the fourth, fifth, and sixth) whose windows look onto the Patio of Masks, display Italian, Spanish and Dutch paintings mainly from the 17th century. Worth noting are *The Journey of Jacob* by Andrea di Leoni in the fourth room;The Two *Still Lifes* by Juan van der Hamen in the fifth; and in the sixth, *Lot Intoxicated by his Daughters* by Guercino.

(7) The seventh room, the former Gallery of Walks of the Summer Palace, with excellent views of the gardens and Madrid, houses some of the most famous canvasses conserved in the Monastery which are also strongly linked to the history of its foundation, such as the ones originally chosen of the Basilica's main altar and later discarded.

These are *The Annunciation* by Veronese, *The Adoration of the Shepherds* by Tintoretto, and *The Nativity* and *The Epiphany* by Federico Zuccaro.

Facing, the great works of the painter Juan Fernández de Navarrete, the Dumb are of interest, such as *The Beheading of St. James* and *St. Jerome Repentant*. Between these two paintings, you can find the excellent copy by Coxcie of *The Descent*, the original of which (previously in El Escorial and now in the Prado Museum) was painted by the 15th century Flemish artist, Van der Weyden, the author of *The Calvary*, which is hung on the front wall of the same room. *The Calling of St. Peter and St. Andrew* by the Italian Federico Barocci is on the opposite wall.

Paolo Cagliari,, the Veronese:
The Anunciation .

Juan Fernández de Navarrete, the Dumb: *The Beheading of St. James* .

Roger van der Weyden :
The Calvary.

The Patio of Masks.

(8) The eighth room is dedicated to 17th century Spanish painting. You can admire here works by José de Ribera, the "Españoleto", the leading figure of the 17th century Neopolitan school, although he was born in Valencia: *Apparition of the Child to St. Anthony,* a *St. Jerome Repentant* and two sculptures, *Crisipo* and *Esopo.*

(9) The ninth room - originally Philip II's summer bedroom leading onto the gallery of the "underground church" which he used as private chapel, and which is now the Pantheon of the Kings is dedicated to Luca Giordano and some 17th century Spanish painters. Two paintings of the *Virgin with Child* by Alonso Cano are worth noting here.

A corridor from the last room in the Museum of Art leads out to the *Patio of Masks.*

□
■   **2   PATIO OF MASKS**
□

This patio, which is overshadowed by the enormous façade of the Church, owes its name to the two fountains in its eastern wall; the rest of the patio is surrounded by porticos formed by semi-circled arches on Tuscan columns, which is typical of the country house style of this royal residence. In addition to the so obviously inspired Italian design of this patio, a touch of Flemish influence can be noted from the roofs and

The Patio of Masks.

Detail from the *Battle of the Higueruela* in the Gallery of Battles.

the curious chimney tops, which were the only part of this building left untouched by the terrible fire of 1671, the *House of the King,* which is built around the patio on two floors, with the summer rooms on the ground floor and the winter rooms on the main one.

■
□ **3** THE GALLERY OF BATTLES
□

From the maskes patio, the Queen staircase goes to the Gallery of Battles, located in the main floor of the public palace. This vast hall 55 meters long is covered in frescoes depicting war scenes (hence the name) painted by Fabrizio Castello, Orazio Cambiasso and Lazzaro Tavarone. These "long works", as they are known, were typical of that period and were used for covered walks as well as for solemn receptions.

Here, Philip II wanted to demonstrate the connection between is campaigns for European hegemony and the bellicose attitude of the Spanish Christian monarchs of the Middle Ages. The *Battle of Higueruela,* John II of Castile's victory over the natives of Granada in 1431, painted on the long wall facing the windows (it is a copy of a long 15th century sketch found in the Alcázar of Segovia) is set off against several scenes depicted on the front walls and the walls between the balconies. These are of the *Battle of San Quentin* from the Portuguese campaign, and the clashes with the English in the Azores, which all took place during Philip II's reign.

■
□ **4** THE HOUSE OF THE KING
□

Descending once again, on the Queen's staircase, we reach the main floor of the "House of the King" private palace, which individuality inside of the Monastery is evident by the disposition of its floors,in intermediate levels, in respec to the rest of the group. The House of the King is symbolically located in the central axis of the building, and is joined closely to the sanctuary in such a fashion that the figure of the King appears as if protected by Divine Grace and as defender of the Faith; mediator between the sacred and the profane (Monastery and Palace), but at the same time separated from

General view of
the Gallery of Bat-
tles. Fresco pain-
tings by Granello,
Castello, Cambias-
so and Tavarone.

The King's chapel seen from the Basilica.

The Infanta's bedroom.

mere mortals by these rooms where "no-one without license can enter, like an eagle in its eyrie". The House of the King is, despite its modest size and appearance, the centre of the entire Monastery, since from here, the Sacred Monarch had access to all parts of the Monastery.

As all the palaces of the Spanish Monarchs of that time, this one at El Escorial was divided into two similarly laid-out chambers for both the *King* and the *Queen* They were situated in such a fashion that they could see through the adjoining private chapel and from their respective bedrooms the high altar of the church. "Luckily the monarchs were lodged within and yet outside the main chapel, the design of which would not have been more dignified or more great". The Queen's chamber is attributed the highest honour by being located on the side of the Evangel (on the left, if one looks towards the altar); as the King became a widower for the fourth and last time in 1580, the Queen's chamber was used by her daughter, Isabel Clara Eugenia, which is why it is named the *Chamber of the Infanta.*

From the staircase we reach the *Ante-chamber,* and from this to the Chamber or bedroom of the female infant. The chancel of the church can be seen from this chamber and the *Gardens of the Queen* from the windows.

The portrait of *Isabel Clara Eugenia* by Bartolomé González hangs next to her sister's, *Catalina Micaela* from the Sánchez Coello school. The small *hand organ* is from the 16th century.

General view of the Hall of Portraits.

Inlaid German door in the Gallery of
Walks.

Antonio Moro : *Philip II.*

General view of the King's
Gallery of Walks.

You return to the Ante-Chamber by going around the corridors above the Patio of Masks which join the King's chamber with the Queen's. This *Ante-Chamber* is decorated with various paintings by Juan Correa de Vivar and from the Bassano studio. Philip II's *hand chair* is also found in this chamber.

The chair, whish was used by the gout-ridden King in the last years of his life, has a curious system for dismantling the back. The structure allowed for a canopy to be placed on top and the sides closed off.

You then come to the *King's Quarters*. The sequence of distribution and use of the rooms were governed in the Spanish royal palaces by Burgundian etiquette, imposed by Charles V, which reinforced the "sacred" identity of the Monarch: each room has a successively more restricted entrance, depending on the visitor's rank.

The Talavera tiled frieze covering the lower part of the walls is original. In general, the furnishing of these rooms reflects what is known today as 16th century decoration.

Chinese folding chair used by
Philip II.

From the Ante-Chamber, you reach the *Hall of Portraits,* which owes its name to the royal portraits of the House of

The King's Quarter or Ante-Chamber.

Austria exhibited there. They are the works of Pantoja de la Cruz, Sánchez Coello, Antonio Moro and Juan Carreño.

This room was used for common audiences with the King. The Chinese fold-able chairs from the Ming era (second half of the 16th century) were used by the King to rest his gouty leg. A fine example is the Antonio Moro portrait of *Philip II* at the age of 35, believed to be dressed in the armour of the *Battle of San Quentin.*

From the Hall of portraits along the Gallery of Walks to the King's Chamber, you pass through two wooden inlaid doors "of the best and best carved to come to us from Germany, expertly designed", sent as a gift by the Emperor Maximilian II to Philip II in 1567.

The Gallery of Walks, inside the King's Chamber, was a typical feature of 16th century European palaces which served for indoor strolls when the weather was bad.

Father Sigüenza furnished more or less all of the paintings of military scenes (with Flemish landscapes) from Philip II's epoch and the 16th century engraved maps hung in this gallery. The *meridians*, on the floor of this room and the next, are the work of Father Wedlingen (1755).

The two interior rooms parallel to this gallery looking out onto the Patio of

The King's Chamber.

"Watchtower" by Hans
of Evalo, 1583.

Masks, which can be seen from the doors, are decorated with paintings from the 16th and 17th centuries.

In the *King's Chamber* or *the Ante-Chamber*, there is a complete series of 17th century anonymous paintings of Philip II's royal residences around Madrid. This series demonstrates the taste for architecture and passion for building of the Sovereign, even while he was still the Prince. His greatest architectural achievement is undoubtedly the El Escorial Monastery, of which some engravings by Pedro Perret, based on designs by Juan de Herrera, are also exhibited.

This series is fundamental for an understanding of the building. These engravings were here in Philip II's time in addition to "still life paintings of many things found in our New World: some of the many different species of fowl .. others of a great variety of large and small animals ... and others thousand insects."

By crossing a corridor that encircles the *King's staircase,* you reach *Philip II's bedchamber,* where he died on September 13th, 1598:

"..in the same house and temple of San Lorenzo that had built himself, almost above his own tomb, at five o'clock in the morning, when the dawn was

The King's Chamber, with the study and the bedroom. In the background, the chapel.

breaking in the East ...the seminary children were singing the dawn mass, the last mass they gave for his health, and the first for his salvation."

The position of his bed, which had been inspired by his father's bed in Yuste, allowed the King to see, from his bedside, the countryside through the two balconies and, on the other side, his chapel and the Basilica's high altar. On the table in the study, there is a "watchtower" - the work of Philip II's clockmaker, the German, Hans of Evalo.

Signed in 1583, it is a typical mannerist piece. The Monarch used only the light of his little oil lamp when he wrote at night. The King's Bedchamber was decorated in its day with works by Bosch, now in the Prado Museum. Among the paintings exhibited today in the bedchamber are *Virgin with the child and saints* by Benvenuto Tisi, il Garofolo; a *Pietà* by Gerard David and *The Portrait of Philip II* as an old man by Pantoja de la Cruz. The ebony, silver and bronze retable is a Roman piece by Antonio Gentili following the design of Giuliano della Porta, and was a gift from the Great Duchess of Tuscany to the King in 1586. The rest of the paintings, all on pious themes, are Flemish and German from the early 16th century.

Two fine examples of agate paintings by Annibale Carracci are found in the cupboard, as well as several medieval gold and silver objects from the 16th century.

The austerity of these chambers is quite surprising given the royal pomp and splendour of the Modern Age and the fact that Philip II, King of Spain and the New World, was the most important European Monarch of the century. Nonetheless, one must take into account that this was the "Royal Chamber" of the Monastery's founder inside the building itself in which Philip II, following the medieval tradition, used to live and cultivate his religious and filial piousness.

Leaving these rooms, you go down a corridor that leads to the *Ante-Sactristy* from where the *Main Cloister* is reached.

☐
☐
■   **5 THE PANTHEONS**

One of El Escorial's main functions is the burial place for the Spanish Monarchs. Nevertheless, this did not materialize until after the founder's death, who had said, according to biographical notes, that he had built a dwelling place for God; and that his son, if he so wished, could do so for his bones, and then the bones of his father. The two Pantheons reflect two distinct styles and centuries: the barroque style of the 17th century for the *Kings and Queens,* and the eclectic 19th century for the Infantes or their children.

The Pantheons are reached by a stairway which stems from the church to the Sacristy. The left branch leads to the Pantheons of the Kings and the right to the Infantes'.

The *Pantheons of the Kings* is a dome-covered circular chamber whose circumference is divided into eight sections. Juan de Herrera conceived and built it in granite, but when Philip III decided to convert it into a Pantheon, he had the overseer of the royal constructions, Giovanni Battista Crescenzi, surface it in marble and bronze, according to a project by Juan Gómez de Mora begun in 1617. The work was prolonged because of difficulties that arose throughout almost all of Philip IV's reign, and was not completed until 1654.

Crescenzi, a Roman, directed the work done in bronze, carried out by Italian, in particular, Genovese artesans. The marble work was led by Pedro de Lizargárate and Bartolomé Zumbigo, the Elder. It was during Philip IV's reign that the solution to the technical problems was found (a spring had appeared when the floor was

Entrance door to the Pantheon of the Kings.

Altar from the Pantheon of the Kings.

The sixth chamber of the Pantheon of the Infantes.

General view of the
Pantheon of the Kings.

33

The tomb of Juan de Austria, in the fifth chamber of the Pantheon of the Infantes.

lowered), along with the addition of grotesques to the dome, the new floor design and all the surfacing of the stairway and its doors, the gilding of the bronzes and the inclusion of some more. The richness of the marble (the blue-tint from Toledo and the red from Tortosa) and the bronze, the Corinthian pomp and the exuberant baroque of the grotesques make this chamber a fine example of early Italian baroque, giving it a more international than Spanish air. Presiding over the altar is a *Christ Crucified* by Domenico Guidi, a less well-known artist, but more fortunate that Gian Lorenzo Bernini and Pietro Tacca who had previously produced other crucifixes for the same altar, but which are now kept in the College chapel and in the Sacristy vestry respectively.

The remains (after having previously laid for years in an adjoining temporary vault, the "Pudridero") of the monarchs and their wives lie in the urns, that is, only the wives who had born their husbands children; the kings on the right and the queens on the left, placed in chronological order from Charles I to Alphonse XIII, which spans a period of four centuries of the Spanish Monarchy.

The *Pantheon of the Infantes* was built on the orders of Isabella II, based on a project by José Segundo de Lema, and was completed in 1888. Each of the nine chambers, located beneath the Sacristy and the Chapter Houses, are presided over by an altar and surfaced in marble. The sculptures and adornments were produced in Carrara by Jacobo Baratta di Leopoldo modelled on work by Ponciano Ponzano. The style of this Pantheon, inspired for historical reasons, gives rise to some new and truly funereal architectural forms. The cold aspect, the historic interest and the 19th century spirit pervading the Pantheon all add to its richness and attraction.

The most outstanding of the nine rooms are: first chamber: neoclasic altar with a Descend of Carlo Veronese, tombs of María Josefa de Borbón, by Isidro G. Veázquez, of the mother in law of Isabel II, Luisa Carlota de Borbób, the Dukes of Monpensier, and that of their daughters by Aimé Millet. The *fifth chamber,* contains the sepulchre of D. Juan de Austria, which is the work of Giuseppe Galeotti following the design of Ponzano. The *sixth chamber* is occupied by a mausoleum of the Kings' children who died before reaching puberty, which resembles a sort of twenty-sided tart in white marble. On the altar, there is a fine painting by Lavinia Fontana (1590). The *ninth chamber* has the most historical interest as it contains sixteen tombs pertaining to the House of Austria.

José de Ribera : *St. Francis of Assisi.*

Detail from the ceiling of the Chapter Houses.

At the far end of the Pantheon of the Infantes, you find two arched cellars called the "silversmiths' workshops" form which a stairway leads up to the *Chapter Houses.*

☐
■ **6 THE CHAPTER HOUSES**
☐

These rather impressive and large Chapter Houses surrounded by a wooden bench were designed for the assemblies of the one hundred monks that lived in the Monastery. Two rooms are separated by a central entrance hallway: the *Vicarial* and the *Prioral*, whose names come from the vicar or prior who presided over them. The last square room beneath the tower is the lower *Priory Cell*. These Chapter Houses, the Priory Cell and the entrance hallway form a magnificient row of four rooms, whose vaulted ceilings are painted with frescoes with grotesque motifs by Fabrizio Castello and Nicola Granello. Most of the canvasses that used to hang on the walls are now part of the Prado Museum collection and the remaining works are also fine examples of art.

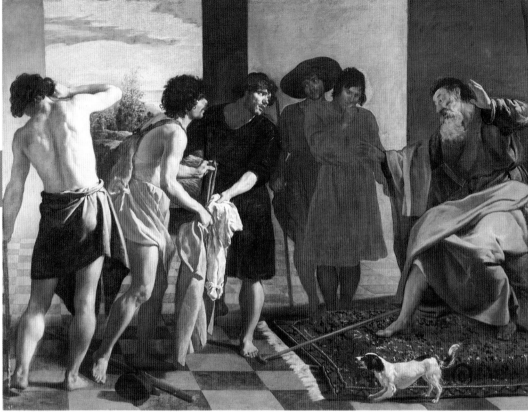

Diego Velázquez : *The Tunic of Joseph.*

Pride of place in the *Vicarial Room* is Tiziano's *St. Jerome Repentant*. Alongside are the two *flower paintings* by Mario Nuzzi, called "dei fiori", and the two eremite saints, *St. Paul and St. Jerome* by José de Ribera, who also painted the three magnificent canvasses hanging on the long wall facing the windows: *St. Francis Receiving the Stigmata, Jacob with his Flock* and *a Pietà*. One of the Spanish masters's works is also exhibited here: Diego Velázquez's *The Tunic of Joseph*, painted during his first stay in Rome. Some of El Greco's most celebrated works hang between the window. They are *The Adoration of the Name of Jesus* which is an allegory of the painting The Holy Alliance of Philip II, the Pope and Venice against the Turks in 1571.

36

The *Prioral Room* is mainly decorated with Venetian art: Tiziano's *The Rest on the Flight to Egypt* and *The Last Supper* which was, unfortunately, cut down to size to fit on the wall; Tintoretto's *The Lavatory* and *Esther before Asuero;* Veronese's *The Apparition of Christ to the Virgin with the Parents of Limbo* and Moretto da Brescia's *The Eritrean Prophetress* and *The Prophet Isaias.*

Tiziano : *The Last Supper.*

The Gospel lecterns, the work of Juan Simon de Amberes in 1571, are exhibited in the centre of the room. In the *Priory Cell,* there is still a collection of Hyeronimus Bosch's, known in Spain as "El Bosco", board paintings, which include *The Calvary Way, The Haycart* and *Paradise.* Above the altar, you can see the *portable retable of Emperor Charles V,* which is a splendid example of enamelled and wooden gold-plated silver put together by different workshops. The relief work and the apostles are more Italianized and the three apexes are of a later and more international mannerist style.

☐ ■ 7 THE MAIN CLOISTER ☐

The Main Cloister galleries around the Patio of the Evangelists are decorated with forty-six frescoes depicting the *Story of the Redemption* from the birth of the Virgin until the Last Judgement. They go in order from the Procession Door, which joins the Cloister with the church. This series is painted

El Greco: *The Adoration of the Name of Jesus*, otherwise known as "The dream of Philip II".

Portable altar of Emperor Charles V,

by Pellegrino Tibaldi and his studio. The "stations" in the corners are by Luis de Carvajal, Cincinnato, Tibaldi, Luis de Carvajal and Miguel Barroso.

Next, it is a good idea to take a turn around the galleries to admire the paintings and the *Temple of the Evangelists*

☐
■   **A** THE PATIO OF THE EVANGELISTS
☐

This is one of the most interesting areas in the building from an architectural point of view as much for the gallery façades of the Cloister, based on a Juan Bautista de Toledo design modified by Juan de Herrera, as for the Temple (the work of Herrera) and which gives the patio its name.

The patio garden, laid out in a typically cloistered style - in the shape of a cross - is encircled by a Doric building in allusion not only to the fountain of Grace

The Cloister Gallery.

Exterior view of the Cloister Galleries and the Patio of the Evangelists. Church by Juan de Herrera, with sculptures by Juan Bautista Monegro.

and spiritual life (the Four Gospels), but also to the Garden of Eden with the four rivers which irrigate the four corners of the world: this Temple of the Evangelists was designed in 1586 by Juan de Herrera; the sculptures are by Juan Bautista Monegro.

■ 8 THE MAIN STAIRCASE

The main staircase is found in the centre of the western gallery of the Cloister. This "impressive and beautiful" staircase was not based on Juan Bautista de Toledo designs, but was apparently the work of Gian Battista Castello, known as the Bergamasco. Added to its attractive architectural design is the lavishness of the fresco ceiling painted in 1692 by Luca Giordano: *The Glory of the Spanish Monarchy.* Charles II, depicted in the centre of the western wall, is showing this apotheosis to his mother, Mariana of Austria and to his wife Mariana of Neoburg.

There are a few more places of interest around the Cloister, like the *Old Church* and the *Sacristy*, but they are closed to the public.

■ 9 THE OLD CHURCH

This Old Church was on loan, that is to say, it served as a temporary worship place for the monks form 1571 until the Basilica was completed in 1586. The three very impressive marble retables are conserved in their original state. On the biggest retable, you can see one of Tiziano's masterpieces: the magnificent *Martyrdom of St. Lawrence,* a replica of which is found in the "dei Gesuiti" church in Venice.

A door in the northeastern corner of the galleries leads to the Ante-Sacristy chamber which joins the Pantheons to the Church and the Cloister.

■ 10 THE SACRISTY

Despite being closed to the public, this vast rectangular hall is worth mentioning for several reasons. Its ceiling is painted with grotesques by Granello and Castello. The paintings on its walls are some of the best in the Monastery, and you can still find an odd treasure or two, such as Tiziano's *Christ Crucified, a St. Peter* by Ribera and several canvasses by

Claudio Coello : detail from *The Adoration of the Holy Ghost by Charles II.*

General view of the Sacristy, with the altar of the Holy Ghost in the background.

Lucas Jordán : *The Glory of the Spanish Monarchy.* St. Lawrence and St. Jerome act on the behalf of Charles V and Philip II before the Trinity. In the frieze, there are scenes of the *Battle of San Quentin* and the building of the Monastery.*

41

General view of the Basilica
from the upper passageways.

Giordano. The finest example is the masterpiece painted by the head of the Madrid school after Velázquez's death, and Claudio Coello's *The Adoration of the Holy Ghost by Charles II*, in which barroque ingenuity gives imaginary depth to the sacristy scene and depicts the ceremony just as it was celebrated in this very room in October, 1684 - a true snapshot of the Spanish Court. This painting has an anecdotal tale to tell as it also serves as a screen or veil to conceal the chamber of the Holy Ghost to reveal it only on special occasions. And so, the painting actually descends, sliding down the railings until it disappears from view. The work on the retable and the vestry was based on a José del Olmo design. From the Cloister, you can reach the Basilica Porch and the King's Patio by crossing the *Trinity Room*.

■ 11 THE BASILICA

This great monastic church is the true "raison d'être" of El Escorial. Although Juan Bautista de Toledo set the location and boundaries within his "universal design", they were not his alone which provided the end result, but rather a combined effort, to which Juan de Herrera added a variety of different influences and styles.

Juan Bautista de Toledo's designs included a semi-circular apse flanked by towers; the engineer-architect, Franceso Paciotto, strongly criticized its general proportions in 1562 and suggested in 1563 a square-shaped design. Toledo developed another project in 1567 and, from this year on until 1572, Philip II had the best Italian architects present their plans, which were examined, along with the Spanish projects, by the Florentine Academy and by Vignola in Rome. After studying all the plans in 1573, he decided they were not what he was looking for and did not make his decision until 1574. Philip II finally opted, apparently due to Herrera's influence, for Paciotto's project. The final result is similar to the Genovese church of Santa Maria of Carignano by G. Alessi. The organizing skills of Juan de Herrera and the overseer, Brother Antonio de Villacastín, excelled in the construction work.

The Basilica really consists of two churches: the people's church, or the *Sotocoro*, and the Royal chapel and the monastic church which make up the main body.

The ground plan of the Sotocoro is a repeat, on a smaller scale, of the high church, whose central area is covered by a rather daring flat cupola. Two altars on each side of the central arch were used for giving mass to the town people. Between this area and the Royal Chapel there is the *Seminarists' Choir* area, which is separated by large bronze railings cast by Tujarón in Saragossa.

On the same level as the main floor above the Sotocoro, you can find the *Monks' Choir* area, which is closed to the public; the cabinet work on the chairs and the organ cases were by the Genovese, José Flecha. One of the 124 chairs located in the southwest corner is slightly wider than the others: it was used by Philip II to listen to the service in the Choir area. The fresco on the cupola, *The Glory*, was painted by Luca Cambiasso, known in Spain as Luqueto.

Several portraits are painted here, such as the one of the artist himself and the overseer, Villacastín. The paintings on the walls were completed by Romulo Cincinnato.

Before going through the bronze railings, your attention is drawn to the *High Chapel*, with its enormous high altarpiece at the back and the *royal cenotaphs* at the sides, according to a canonical classic design by Juan de Herrera. All the gilded

Interior of the Basílica.

View of the ceilings and the dome of the Basílica.

The Choir area, with the marble, wooden and bronze lectern and the Milanese chandelier from the 17th century. In the background, the Basilica's main retable.

Cenotaph of Philip II, in the Main Chapel of the Basilica.

bronze sculpture work is by the two Milanese artists, Leone and Pompeo Leoni.

Worth noting further inside is the beautiful tiny chapel, the *Tabernacle*, designed by Herrera and built between 1579 and 1586 by Jacome Trezzo with a variety of different Spanish marbles. The two canvasses in the first level of the Basilica and the central canvass of the second are by Pellegrino Tibaldi. The rest are by Federico Zuccaro.

The cenotaphs, of Charles V on the Gospel side (left) and Philip II on the Epistle side (right), are crowned by their respective coat-of-arms. There are three doors situated below the cenotaphs: the nearest one leads from the pulpit to the Sacristy and the Reliquary, and the other two lead onto the small private chapels next to the King and Queen's bedroom.

This arrangement is a copy of the Emperor's quarters in Yuste. It is also meant that Philip II practically slept above his tomb, and prayed below the place appointed for his own burial statue. Philip II is surrounded by his wives: Isabella of Valois, María of Portugal (the mother of Prince Charles who is at her side) and Ana of Austria. Opposite, next to an armed Charles V wearing the royal mantle, is the Empress Isabella (Philip II's mother); behind her, her daughter, María; and next, the Emperor's sisters, María of Hungary and Leonor of France.

The *ceiling of the Presbytery* is decorated, as is the Choir area, with frescoes by Luqueto and depict *The Coronation of the Virgin.* The remaining ceilings were coated with stucco in the 16th century, and in 1693, Charles II had Luca Giordano decorate them with frescoes giving an impressive barroque appearance.

Giordano is known in Spain as Lucas Jordán thanks to the great amount of work he did, not only here, but in Naples for Spain. Because of his skill and speed, he was assigned great quantities of work and he was deservedly nick-named "Fa presto" or "the speedy". Giordano painted these ceilings and the one above the Monastery staircase in only 22 months, from September, 1692 to July 1694, when he was 57 years old.

In addition to the large altars-reliquaries painted by Federico Zuccaro, which are situated at the head of the two side aisles (*The Annunciation* and *St. Jerome in the Desert*), there are another *forty retables* adorned with canvasses distributed around the various chapels and recesses of the Basilica,

Leoni : group of sculptures depicting Charles V and his family.

Detail from the cenotaph of Philip II.

45

Benvenuto Cellini : *Christ crucified.*

Lucas Jordán: fresco ceiling, with
The Exodus of the Israelites.

which are the work of Luis de Carvajal, Diego de Urbina and Alonso Sánchez Coello, all of them Spanish, as well as the Italians Luca Cambiasso, Romulo Cincinnato and Pellegrino Tibaldi.

The decoration of the Basilica is completed by the two large bronze candela-brum, *"el tenebrario"* and *"el clavel"*, by Juan Simon de Amberes, around

1571; and the two pulpits by Manuel de Urquiza, commissioned by Ferdinand VII around 1830.

A masterpiece of 16th century Italian sculpture is exhibited in one of the chapels at the foot of the church: the superb *Christ Crucified* in Carrara marble which Benvenuto Cellini scuplted in 1562 to place over his own tomb in the Florentine church of San Lorenzo.

It never occupied this place because the Great Duke of Tuscany persuaded him to sell it to him, and he later gave it to Philip II. Engraved with the author's name and date on the pedestal, the morbid beauty of this nude sculpture is admirable.

The Basilica opens onto the *Patio of Kings* with its beautiful façade, and from here a staircase that ascends from the righthand side leads to the *Library.*

☐
■   **12** PATIO OF KINGS
☐

The Patio of Kings is dominated by the dome and façade of the Basilica.

The sculpture of the six great kings of Judea and that of St. Lawrence, set on a single base, are again by Juan Bautista Monegro. All seven figures were sculp-

General view of the Patio of the Kings, with the façade of the Basilica.

Façade of the Library on the Patio of the Kings.

General view of the Library.

tured from the same chunk of stone on which the following message was carved: "six kings and a saint / emerged from the rock / and there was still room for more." The Patio was originally designed by Juan Bautista de Toledo with side porticos, but these were never built. The righthand tower is the watchtower, the lefthand equivalent was named "of the chimes" after a Flemish organ, restored and re-installed in 1988.

13 THE LIBRARY

The original plans of the Monastery contemplated the building of a Library as simply another of the many halls and chambers surrounding the Cloister and it did not gain any special or symbolic significance until much later. Given its location, it serves to connect the Convent quarters to the College, and also combines the role of threshold to the central axis of the building: a sort of crossroads of knowledge, faith and power. In admiring the richness of the decorative work that

Detail from the fresco on the Library ceiling, by Pellegrino Tibaldi.

went into the making of the Library, it becomes quite obvious how much importance Philip II attached to it.

Within the library, the main hall or hall of honour is where books, manufactured with the printing press, are stored. There is another room for printed matter and books that had been banned from circulation. The importance that Philip II, inspired by the outcome of the council of Trent, attached to the Library is in direct proportion to that which he gave to the Seminary and the College as from 1579 onwards. But it was also because of the prestige that a Royal Library lent ot the Spanish Crown, a library which could be considered as the accumulation of knowledge and a "precious store" of original codices.

One of the Library windows.

Over the centuries, many of the books and manuscripts have been lost - a huge fire destroyed part of the collection in 1671-. Nevertheless, the Library still has over 40,000 editions, including an impressive number of Latin, Greek, Arabic and Hebrew manuscripts.

Apart from its store of 4,000 books and manuscripts which belonged to the Crown and which were kept until then in the Royal Chapel of Granada, the King had brought to El Escorial several private collections. Father Sigüenza and Arias Montano were charged with the classification of the immense collection, which was increased during the reign of Philip III by some 4,000 Arabic manuscripts.

Given the number of windows it boasts - seven of which open onto the Patio of Kings and five onto "la Lonja" - the 55 by 10 meter Library is "bright, full of majesty and light". Its shelves are a

One of the Library shelves.

One of the seven identical patios of the College and the Convent.

spectacle in themselves and so too are its frescoes. These last, painted between 1586 and 1593 by Pellegrino Tibaldi in the mannerist style, are clearly influenced by Michelangelo. The complex and extensive iconography which mostly represents or depicts the great wise men of Antiquity, was the brainchild of the chronicler of El Escorial's foundation, Brother José de Sigüenza.

The series of frescoes by Tibaldi begins at the entrance to the College with a representation of Philosophy, and at the far side, the south side or Convent end, with a representation of Theology. Between the two extremes, the visitor can contemplate the sciences, or the seven liberal arts, as organized under the medieval dictum of the Trivium (Grammar, Rhetoric and Dialectics) and that of the Quadrivium (Arithmethic, Music, Geometry and Astrology). These allegoric representations of the arts are situated in separate sections of the ceiling with two learned disciples of each science depicted in the semicircular "windows" on either side. Below the ceiling, the friezes are adorned with yet more references to the particular science depicted directly above.

The finely elaborated *Doric bookcases* were built by José Flecha according to designs by Juan de Herrera. The books are placed with the leaves facing out so the paper could "breathe", their gold-tinted edges peeping through the fine metal meshing which "enhances the whole, since from bottom to top, it seems as if painted with gold".

Library

The shelves themselves, mounted on marble, are carved form Indian-coloured wood, the cane shafts and the base and capitals from orange wood. The tables were sculptured by marble cutter, Bartolomé Zumbigo, the Elder, around 1639.

View of the main façade of the Monastery, dominated by the main entrance.

Other elements of cabinet-work worthy of note include the 18th century *cupboard* which is inlaid with ebony and boxwood and which contains the Library's coin collection. Also of interest is the *barroque portico*. Built in 1622, it leads onto the corridors of the Guesthouse Patio; to the portico staircase which in turn leads to "la Lonja".

14 THE MAIN FAÇADE

The main façade of the Monastery has three porticos. The side porticos, identical in execution, correspond to the College (on the left) and the Convent (on the right).

The Convent's portico does not correspond to its main entrance, but to a ramp which leads on to the food stores and, behind them, to the huge *kitchen* and skylight-roofed patio situated between the for lesser cloisters. The layout is more or

The chapel, in the rooms of fine woods.

Detail from the inlaid work adorned with bronze from the rooms of fine wood.

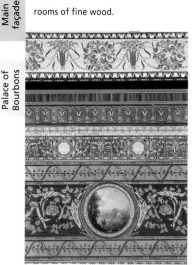

Main façade

Palace of Bourbons

less similar to that of the College, which boasts an aula magna or "theatre".

The main portico, situated in the centre of this façade, leads onto the Monastery and Basilica and is therefore considered to be religiously emblematic in design. It does not, however, bear any relation to the building on which it leans, the library in this case, but rather to the church whose real façade is situated at the end of the atrium.

In fact, Herrera got the inspiration for this façade from an engraving by Serlio, and he was backed in his choice by Philip II himself who was no newcomer to the masteries of architecture. The royal coat-of-arms and the *St. Lawrence* were created by Juan Bautista Monegro.

15 THE PALACE OF THE BOURBONS

By way of the north façade, where our tour began, you enter the Palace of the Bourbons, currently closed to the public. It occupies the eastern and northern sides of the Patio of the Palace or carriages. During the reign of the Austrias, the halls on either side were used by the royal family (the eastern one); and by the courtiers (the northern).

Charles III and Charles IV, and later Ferdinand VII, adapted the halls to better accomodate the royal family. Given the coherence in the decoration, the richness of the tapestries from Madrid's Royal Factory of St. Barbara, it is the most typical of all the Spanish Bourbon palaces.

The access to the Palace is via a staircase built by the architect Juan de Villanueva in 1793. From the higher landing, three passageways lead to the royal chambers. We will follow that which leads the way to the *King's room.*

After crossing three ante-chambers, which are empty today, you come across the *Hall of Audiences,* a curiously decorated room in the neogothic style from the times of Charles IV and which is one of the earliest examples of this kind of art in Spain. The tapestries, designed by Goya, Bayeu and Castillo, came from Madrid's Royal Factory of St. Barbara.

The Hall of Audiences.

Detail from the Palace of the Bourbons.

Next are the so-called *rooms of fine wood*, representative of the culmination of the high international standards reached in inlaywork and decorative arts of Charles IV style. Decorative work on these four rooms - the office, what was called the ante-chamber of the Prie Dieu, private chapel and water closet - contained marbles of Indian wood inlay, and took from 1793

The Garden of the Monks seen from the Gallery of Convalescents or the "Sun Passageways".

to 1831 to complete. The ornamental motifs are inspired in the classicist style, in Pompeian forms and in those of Robert Adam, among other European genuises of the late 18th century. Diverse tendencies are united here in rich and elaborate harmony. From the Hall of Audiences, you come across a series of rooms aligned along the eastern façade.

Seamstresses' chamber, tapestries with Pompeian motifs.
Queen's bedroom, tapestries depicting scenes from Madrid
Dresser, Fernandino styled decor and tapestry depicting foxhunting scenes according to a Castillo design.
King's bedroom, tapestries by Bayeu, Castillo and Barbazza.
Day dining-room, ball games , according to a Goya design.
Music chamber, Charles IV consoles and an English 19th century piano. Tapestries by Goya, Castillo, Bayeu and Teniers. This room opens onto the *chapel.*

After visiting these rooms, you can find another series of chambers which also contain hangings from the Royal Tapestry Factory if yo go back through the series of rooms parallel to the previous one with balconies giving onto the patio.

King's private garden, and Priory Tower.

Teniers tapestry room; a small hallway leads on the **Goya room** which is also decorated with Bayeu tapestries.
Pompeian tapestry room, hangings by José del Castillo.
Ante-bedroom, with tapestries by Teniers, Bayeu and Aguirre.
Telemachus or Neptune room, with tapestries by Anglois.
The chapel, with more tapestries from the Telemachus series, situated in the corner of the patio. From there, another series of rooms face South:**Ambassadors' Salon,** with Bayeu tapestries; the **Ante-chamber,** tapestries by Goya and Bayeu.

The Palace Garden.

The next Ante-chamber is situated off the staircase. Here, there are tapestries imitating the style of Teniers and Wouwermans. The *formal dining-room* boasts a series of magnificent tapestries by Goya, Bayeu and Castillo.

THE GARDENS

At the end of the main façade and down the stairs to "la Lonja", you reach the gallery joining the Monastery and the "Compaña". Below the latter, a door leads onto the Patio of the Chemist, and from there, onto the *Gallery of Convalescents* by Juan Bautista de Toledo.

Palace of Bourbons

Gardens

55

Exterior view of the "Upper House" or the House of the Infante and its gardens, south-west of the Monastery.

Ceiling of the central hall in the House of the Infante.*

"This beautiful example of architecture and brickwork which forms two separated façades in these garderns owes its grace to the unmatching archways." As the name suggests, these "sun passageways" were meant for convalescing monks, while at the same time, they served to conceal the retaining wall and link the garden and "la Lonja".

The *Friars' Garden* is situated in the area between the walls which were built to support the Monastery; the two parallel staircases lead to the *garden*, which is graced with a beautiful *pond* by Francisco de Mora.

THE HOUSE OF THE INFANTE

The so-called House of the Infante or Upper House, was built by Juan de Villanueva between 1771 and 1773 for the Infante Don Gabriel, the son of Charles III. Its noble ionic architecture includes an Italian-styled terraced garden which offers one of the best views of the Monastery.

Gardens

56

Gardens

The austere ground plan of this building, which is dominated by a large high-ceilinged room, was designed for chamber concerts. The entrance, with its framed columns, is a typical characteristic of Villanueva's architecture.

THE HOUSE OF THE PRINCE

The House of the Prince or Lower House, was built around the same time as the House of the Infante for Don Gabriel's elder brother, the future Charles IV, by Juan de Villanueva. It was later en-

Small room with paintings by Lucas Jordán on the ground floor of the House of the Prince.*

larged between 1781 and 1784 by the same architect. As well as being bigger, this House has an advantage over the Infante's in that its interior decoration is in a much better condition.

The architectural design of the House of the Prince (also seen in the House of the Infante, but to a lesser degree) perfectly combines the main building with the smaller ones and its formal garden, which was also designed by Villanueva, but later ruined due to the planting of pine trees in the late 19th and early 20th centuries. Extensions were made to the large drawing room and the oval room, giving the ground plan a T-shape, and to the upper part of the west garden with the addition of the pond. On the ground floor, the "Pompeian" painted ceilings are by Manuel Pérez, Felipe López, Juan Duque and Vicente Gómez. Most of the paintings representing religious, allegorical or mythological scenes are by the Neapolitans, Luca Giordano and Corrado Giaquinto. The piece of furniture worthy of note is the large drawing room table, on Corynthian columns, from the Charles IV period.

From the garden of this house, the Basilica dome can be seen above the Park tree tops. It is 92 metres high, 20 higher than the bell towers and 47 higher than the towers. since enough has been said about the Monastery's "qualities", and since it is customary to inform people about certain of the Monastery's "quantities", someone who did do a count calculated that the whole building had 296 exterior windows, with a total number of 2,600; 1,200 doors, 86 staircases, 88 fountains, 16 patios, 15 cloisters and 9 towers, all within an area of 207 by 161 square meters.

Gardens

BIBLIOGRAPHY

HERRERA, Juan de: Sumario y breve declaración de los diseños y estampas de la fábrica de San Lorenzo el Real del Escorial. Madrid, 1589 (facsímile editions, 1954 and 1978).

SIGUENZA, J. de: Fundación del Monasterio de El Escorial. -libros 3 y 4 de Historia de la Orden de San Jerónimo (Madrid, 1605)-, Ed. Turner, Madrid, 1986.

SANTOS, Francisco de los: Descripción del Real Monasterio de San Lorenzo del Escorial, única maravilla del mundo. Madrid, 1657.

XIMENEZ, Andrés: Descripción del Real Monasterio de San Lorenzo del Escorial: Su magnífico templo, panteón y Palacio. Madrid, 1764.

BERMEJO, Damián: Descripción artística del Real Monasterio de San Lorenzo del Escorial y sus preciosidades después de la invasión de los franceses. Madrid, 1820.

LLAGUNO Y AMIROLA, Eugenio: Noticias de los arquitectos y arquitectura desde su restauración, por don Eugenio Llaguno y Amirola, ilustradas y acrecentadas con notas, adiciones y documentos por don Juan Agustín Cean Bermudez, 4 vols. Madrid, 1829.

QUEVEDO, José de: Historia del Real Monasterio de San Lorenzo. Madrid, 1849.

ROTONDO, Antonio: Historia descriptiva, artística y pintoresca del Real Monasterio de San Lorenzo, vulgarmente llamado de El Escorial. Madrid, 1863.

RUIZ DE ARCAUTE, Agustín: Juan de Herrera, arquitecto de Felipe II. Madrid, 1936.

HENERMANN, Theodor: "El Escorial en la crítica estético-literaria del extranjero, esbozo de una historia de su fama", en El Escorial: Revista de cultura y letras, 1943, pp. 319-341.

LOPEZ SERRANO, M.: Trazas de Juan de Herrera y sus seguidores para el Monasterio de El Escorial. Madrid, 1944.

LORENTE JUNQUERA, Manuel: "La galeria de convalecientes, obra de Juan de Herrera", en AEA, 17, no. 63 (1944), pp. 137-147.

PORTABALES, A.: Los verdaderos artífices de El Escorial y el estilo indebidamente llamado herreriano. Madrid, 1945.

ZUAZO UGALDE, S. de: Los origenes arquitectónicos del Real Monasterio de Sann Lorenzo del Escorial Madrid, 1948.

PORTABALES PICHEL, Amancio: Maestros mayores, arquitectos y aparejadores de El Escorial. Madrid, 1952.

ALVAREZ TURIENZO, Saturnino: El Escorial en las letras españolas. Madrid, 1963.

AA.VV.: Monasterio de San Lorenzo el Real de El Escorial. El Escorial. 1964, 2 volumes.

CHUECA GOITIA, Fernando: Casas reales en monasterios y conventos españoles. Madrid 1966.

TAYLOR, René: "Architecture and Magic: Considerations on the idea of the Escorial", en Essays in the History of Architecture presented to Rudolf y Wittkower, pp. 81 -109, Nueva York, 1967. (Spanish version, Traza y Baza, 6, pp. 5-62.)

KUBLER, George: Building the Escorial. Princeton 1982. Spanish edition, Alianza Editorial, Madrid 1983.

OSTEN SACKEN, C. Von der: El Escorial, estudio iconológico. Madrid, 1984.

RIVERA BLANCO, J. Javier: Juan Bautista de Toledo y Felipe II. La implantación del clasicismo en España. Universidad de Valladolid, 1984.

AA.VV.: El Escorial en la Biblioteca Nacional, Catalogue of the exposition, IV Centenario Fundación Monasterio de El Escorial, Madrid, 1985-1986. with a very completed bibliography about studies of the monastery and travellers who mention it.

El Escorial: la Arquiectura del Monasterio. COAM, Madrid, 1986.

AA.VV.: El Escorial. Biografia de una epoca (la historia), catálogo de la exposición, D.G.B.A., Madrid, 1986. With complete bibliography.

AA.VV.: El Escorial (Ideas y Diseño), catálogo de la exposición, M.O.P.U, Madrid, 1986.

MOLEON, Pedro: La arquitectura de Juan de Villanueva. COAM, Madrid, 1988.

GARCIA-FRIAS CHECA, Carmen: La decoración de la Biblioteca del Monasterio de El Escorial. Patrimonio Nacional, Madrid 1990.

RUIZ GOMEZ, Leticia: Catálogo de la colección de pintura veneciana histórica del Monasterio de El Escorial. Patrimonio Nacional, Madrid 1991

CHECA CREMADES, Fernando: Felipe II, mecenas de las artes, Madrid 1992.

MULCAHY, Rosemary: A mayor gloria de Dios y del Rey. La decoración de la Basílica de El Escorial. Patrimonio Nacional, 1992.

Revistas Reales Sitios (Patrimonio Nacional), La Ciudad de Dios (PP. Agustinos).

THE PRINTING OF THIS BOOK, PUBLISHED JOINTLY BY THE PATRIMONIO NACIONAL AND ALDEASA, WAS FINISHED ON THE 24 TH DAY OF AUGUST, 1997 FESTIVITY OF SAN SERGIO AT ESTUDIOS GRÁFICOS EUROPEOS, MADRID.